ORIGIN STORIES

LORE AND

XIII

LEGENDS

BY
JEN BREACH

ILLUSTRATED BY
JOSHUA JANES

Rourke.

BEFORE AND DURING READING ACTIVITIES

Before Reading: *Building Background Knowledge and Vocabulary*

Building background knowledge can help children process new information and build upon what they already know. Before reading a book, it is important to tap into what children already know about the topic. This will help them develop their vocabulary and increase their reading comprehension.

Questions and Activities to Build Background Knowledge:

1. Look at the front cover of the book and read the title. What do you think this book will be about?
2. What do you already know about this topic?
3. Take a book walk and skim the pages. Look at the table of contents, photographs, captions, and bold words. Did these text features give you any information or predictions about what you will read in this book?

Vocabulary: *Vocabulary Is Key to Reading Comprehension*

Use the following directions to prompt a conversation about each word.

- Read the vocabulary words.
- What comes to mind when you see each word?
- What do you think each word means?

Vocabulary Words:
- crones
- lore
- pagan
- stingy
- superstitions
- threshold

During Reading: *Reading for Meaning and Understanding*

To achieve deep comprehension of a book, children are encouraged to use close reading strategies. During reading, it is important to have children stop and make connections. These connections result in deeper analysis and understanding of a book.

Close Reading a Text

During reading, have children stop and talk about the following:

- Any confusing parts
- Any unknown words
- Text to text, text to self, text to world connections
- The main idea in each chapter or heading

Encourage children to use context clues to determine the meaning of any unknown words. These strategies will help children learn to analyze the text more thoroughly as they read.

When you are finished reading this book, turn to the next-to-last page for **After-Reading Questions** and an **Activity**.

Table of Contents

A Legend's Beginning

Lean in.

Listen carefully.

To the legends behind the stories you already know.

You've heard of Halloween and fear and fright?
Of witches on brooms who swoop and scare?
Of curses that bring bad luck and loss?

But where did these tales come from?
If you're quiet, I will tell you the origin stories.

But you must be quiet.

The witches might be listening ...

What if there was a barrier between our world and the spirit world? A barrier that was thinner than tissue paper. And on one day a year ...

it was even thinner than that.

Many cultures around the world observe days like that. They are called **threshold** festivals.

It's when we who are alive are thought to be able to communicate with our loved ones who have died. On days like the Jewish holiday Yom Kippur, the Chinese Hungry Ghost Festival, and Mexico's Day of the Dead, or *Dia de los Muertos*, people remember and celebrate their dead relatives.

But for those who celebrate Halloween, the main concern is keeping those from the other side out.

BOO!

HALLOWEEN TRAITS

🌙 Pagan

👻 Costumes

💀 Death-centered

🍬 Treats

The first record of Samhain, or Halloween, comes from the 9th century, but it was practiced for many centuries before that!

GEOGRAPHIC LOCATIONS

UNITED STATES

SCOTLAND

IRELAND   WALES

EUROPE

MEXICO

CHINA

pagan (PAY-guhn): a person who isn't part of the Jewish, Muslim, or Christian religions. They may have multiple gods or not practice religion

threshold (THRESH-hohld): the place or point between two places, like a border

It doesn't look the same anymore, but modern Halloween is based on the ancient Celtic festival, Samhain. In Celtic **lore**, the human world and spirit world collide on Samhain ... but it wasn't a happy day to remember loved ones who had passed. For Celts, the other world is full of spirits and wicked fairies that cause mischief and grief. On Samhain, you protect yourself from their pranks.

Celts kept themselves safe in ways that might sound familiar. They wore costumes to fool the spirits into thinking they were one of them. They left out food and drink to satisfy unwelcome phantoms. They traveled in small groups—never alone. Centuries later, small groups might go from house to house to perform songs or tricks in exchange for coins, nuts, and fruit.

lore (lor): traditional knowledge or beliefs

Fast forward to the 18th century. Early American colonies were settled by millions of immigrants. They came from all over. Some brought Samhain, which had merged over the years with Christian practices and had been renamed Halloween.

But it wasn't until the 1950s that it became the Halloween we recognize today. Candy companies saw an opportunity to boost sweet sales. They marketed Halloween as a candy-based tradition. They had as much impact on modern Halloween as fairies had on Samhain!

And the rest is (commercial) history.

Early Irish immigrants who came to America also brought the practice of carving jack-o'-lanterns.

According to Irish myth, long ago a man called **Stingy** Jack tricked the devil into not claiming his soul when he died. But he couldn't get into Heaven when he died because he had lived a wicked life. And the devil kept his word and turned Stingy Jack's soul away from Hell. So Jack set off into the dark with only a lantern carved out of a turnip to light the path of his doomed wandering.

For centuries, Irish people carved scary faces into turnips and potatoes and lit the lanterns to scare away Stingy Jack and other wicked, restless souls. In the US, the best thing for carving jack-o'-lanterns were ... you guessed it ...

pumpkins!

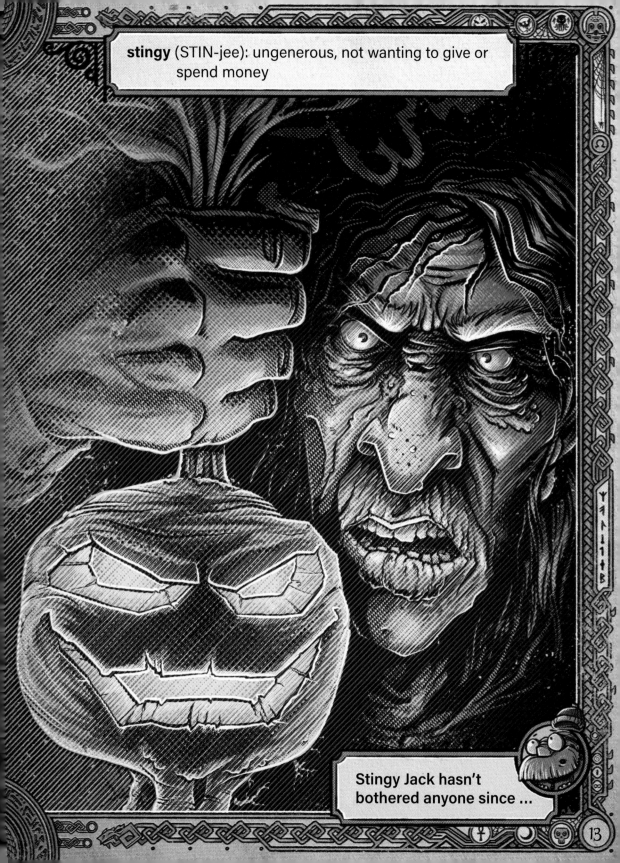

stingy (STIN-jee): ungenerous, not wanting to give or spend money

Stingy Jack hasn't bothered anyone since …

⟡ SUPERSTITIONS ⟡

You've probably had good days where everything went right ...

and bad days where everything went wrong.

But that's what's tricky about luck. It's all up to chance. Or is it? What if you could make sure you had more good days than bad? This desire is why luck practices are common in mythology, folklore, and **superstitions** all over the world. The origins of some of the practices are so old many of the original meanings have been lost to time.

But that doesn't stop us from believing in them ...

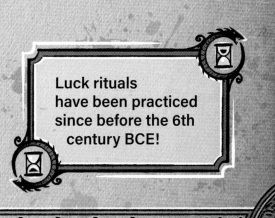

Luck rituals have been practiced since before the 6th century BCE!

SUPERSTITION TRAITS

🍀 Based in luck/chance   ✨ Magic elements

GEOGRAPHIC LOCATIONS

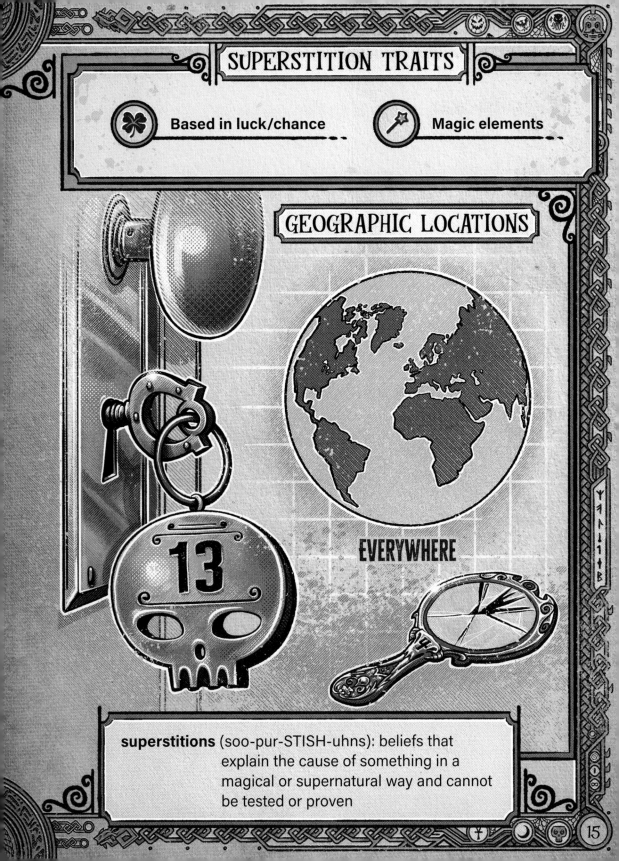

EVERYWHERE

superstitions (soo-pur-STISH-uhns): beliefs that explain the cause of something in a magical or supernatural way and cannot be tested or proven

Break a mirror, be cursed with bad luck. This common belief likely dates back to the ancient Greeks or Romans. For both, reflections held mysterious power. There was a belief that one's reflection had a connection with the soul. Before mirrors, it wasn't often someone would see their own reflection.

When mirrors were created, they became objects of mystery and value. Some people even started telling fortunes using mirrors. All of this likely contributed to the idea that the mirror was an object to respect. You can understand now why breaking one was considered very bad!

Numbers have been long associated with deeper meanings. This includes some unlucky numbers you probably know. The number 13 frightens many. The true reason remains unknown, but there are many theories. One is from Norse mythology, in which the trickster god Loki becomes the 13th guest at dinner and causes the death of another god. Another also comes to us from a dinner party but has Christian origins. Jesus holds the Last Supper before he is killed. Judas, who betrays him, is the 13th guest.

But unlucky numbers vary depending on where you live. Like the number 13, the number 4 holds an unlucky place in many Asian countries. Buildings in China and Japan, especially hospitals, do not have a fourth floor. This is because the word 'four' sounds like the word 'death.'

·WITCHES·

In the dead of night.

In the dark of the woods.

A shadow flies across the bright white moon.

A shadow ...

of a woman ... riding a broomstick.

You hear the wind rustling the dried leaves.

It sounds almost like a cackle ...

This image may look familiar. But that's not how witches started out. Witches appear in folklore and religious traditions from all over the world. Though the stories have witches with different features, practices, and intentions, a common idea of a witch starts to take form. Often the witches were old **crones**. Always they were outsiders, and usually left alone.

The first witch in literature appears in the 8th century BCE.

WITCH TRAITS

- **?** Outsider
- **✦** Magical
- **♀** Often women

GEOGRAPHIC LOCATIONS

UNITED STATES

EAST SLAVIC REGION

ENGLAND

ITALY

JAPAN

crones (krohnz): ugly old women; witch-like women

What legends shaped the witch?

One of the most famous witches in folklore is Baba Yaga. In East Slavic traditions, she is an immortal old woman who lives in the forest in a hut that can walk with its chicken legs. She can fly around in an oversized stone bowl and wipes away her tracks with a broom. She's a trickster figure, sometimes helping but sometimes hurting, her true nature a mystery.

In Japanese folklore, the witch called Yama-Uba can appear in different forms: as a beautiful young woman, a mountain man, a river goddess, a woman in clothes made of bark, or a crone. But the crone is her true identity. Like Baba Yaga, there are stories of Yama-Uba helping some. But she is best known for stealing and eating children.

Very old witches like Baba Yaga or Yama-Uba come from pagan cultures. But in the early Middle Ages, Christianity became popular, and many pagan stories were folded into Bible stories.

The Befana was a pagan witch in Italian folklore. But she's also associated with the Christian birth story of Jesus. Among other mischief, she rode a broom and gave gifts to good children and coal to bad children.

So why the green skin? That's from the 1939 film *The Wizard of Oz*. If the Wicked Witch wore an eyepatch like she does in the book, our Halloween costumes would look pretty different!

These legends all set up the idea that witches were primarily women. Women who lived alone. Women on the edges of society. This wasn't a problem until the Middle Ages when Christians started seeing witches as people to be hunted and killed. Across Europe, more than 40,000 people were killed for practicing witchcraft. In most cases, there was no evidence. And in most cases, they were women.

In 1640, a man named Matthew Hopkins became the Witchfinder General in England. Before Hopkins, witch trials were rare and almost never ended in death. But Hopkins killed more than 300 women in just two years. He even wrote a guidebook for spotting and trying witches. It was used as the handbook for the Salem Witch Trials in the US, and countless other crimes against women on the margins of society.

The last recorded witch trial was in Tennessee in 1883.

The term "witch hunt" is now used to describe the attempt to punish people who have unpopular views.

•THE STORY OF US•

Stories change over time.

Sometimes the changes are small and subtle. Sometimes the story is rewritten from top to bottom.

Remembering where stories come from and understanding why they changed can tell you another story. A story about us. They might reflect shifting beliefs or social norms. They might show you how cultures merged together … or stole from one another.

For better or worse, stories change.

And so do we.

Memory Game

Look at the pictures. What do you remember reading on the pages where each image appeared?

INDEX

AFTER–READING QUESTIONS

1. Where do we get the idea that witches are green-skinned?

2. Before pumpkins, what were jack-o'-lanterns carved out of?

3. What pagan festival became Halloween?

4. Do you believe in any superstitions? Why or why not?

5. When does the Befana visit children in Italy?

ACTIVITY

Beliefs and folklore change over time. Write about how we might think about witches in one hundred years' time. Or write about a potential future superstition.

About the Author

Jen Breach (they/them) knocks on wood every day. They would very much like to meet a real witch. Jen has worked as a bagel-baker, a code-breaker, a ticket-taker and a trouble-maker. They now work as a writer, the best job ever, in Philadelphia, PA.

About the Illustrator

Joshua Janes trained in narrative art at the Joe Kubert School in New Jersey and followed his love of monsters to an illustration career of over 27 years. From his studio in Ohio, his imagination continues to pour forth with the support of his incredible wife, Angie, and their children, Gabi, Bailey, and Cole, along with their bulldog, Pudge.

www.rourkebooks.com

Edited by: Hailey Scragg
Cover and interior illustrations by: Joshua Janes

Library of Congress PCN Data

Lore and Legends / Jen Breach
(Origin Stories)
 ISBN 978-1-73165-740-4 (hard cover) (alk. paper)
 ISBN 978-1-73165-727-5 (soft cover)
 ISBN 978-1-73165-753-4 (e-book)
 ISBN 978-1-73165-766-4 (e-pub)
Library of Congress Control Number: 2023942375
Rourke Educational Media
Printed in the United States of America
01-0152411937